LETTERS TO YESENIN

Books by Jim Harrison

Letters to Yesenin

JIM HARRISON

Copper Canyon Press
Port Townsend, Washington

Printed in the United States of America

Cover art: ©iStockphoto.com / Tatiana Sayig

Copper Canyon Press is in residence at Fort Worden State Park in Port Townsend, Washington, under the auspices of Centrum, a gathering place for artists and creative thinkers from around the world, students of all ages and backgrounds, and audiences seeking extraordinary cultural enrichment.

Many of these poems previously appeared in the following volumes: *Letters to Yesenin,* Sumac Press, 1973; *Letters to Yesenin and Returining to Earth,* Sumac Poetry Series Center Publications, 1979; *The Shape of the Journey: New and Collected Poems,* Copper Canyon Press, 1998

LIBRARY OF CONGRESS CATALOGING-IN-PUBLICATION DATA

Harrison, Jim, 1937–

Letters to Yesenin / Jim Harrison.

p. cm.

ISBN 978-1-55659-265-2

I. Title.

PS3558.A67L485 2007

811´.54–dc22

2007020015

COPPER CANYON PRESS

Post Office Box 271

Port Townsend, Washington 98368

www.coppercanyonpress.org

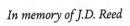

In memory of J.D. Reed

Contents

LETTERS TO YESENIN

1

This matted and glossy photo of Yesenin
bought at a Leningrad newsstand—permanently
tilted on my desk: he doesn't stare at me
he stares at nothing; the difference between
a plane crash and a noose adds up to nothing.
And what can I do with heroes with my brain fixed
on so few of them? Again nothing. Regard his flat
magazine eyes with my half-cocked own, both
of us seeing nothing. In the vodka was nothing
and Isadora was nothing, the pistol waved
in New York was nothing, and that plank bridge
near your village home in Ryazan covered seven feet
of nothing, the clumsy noose that swung the tilted
body was nothing but a noose, a law of gravity
this seeking for the ground, a few feet of nothing
between shoes and the floor a light-year away.
So this is a song of Yesenin's noose that came
to nothing, but did a good job as we say back home
where there's nothing but snow. But I stood under
your balcony in St. Petersburg, yes St. Petersburg!
a crazed tourist with so much nothing in my heart
it wanted to implode. And I walked down to the Neva
embankment with a fine sleet falling and there was

finally something, a great river vastly flowing, flat
as your eyes; something to marry to my nothing heart
other than the poems you hurled into nothing those
years before the articulate noose.

2

to Rose

I don't have any medals. I feel their lack
of weight on my chest. Years ago I was ambitious.
But now it is clear that nothing will happen.
All those poems that made me soar along a foot
from the ground are not so much forgotten as never
read in the first place. They rolled like moons
of light into a puddle and were drowned. Not even
the puddle can be located now. Yet I am encouraged
by the way you hanged yourself, telling me that such
things don't matter. You, the fabulous poet of
Mother Russia. But still, even now, schoolgirls
hold your dead heart, your poems, in their laps
on hot August afternoons by the river while they wait
for their boyfriends to get out of work or their
lovers to return from the army, their dead pets to
return to life again. To be called to supper. You
have a new life on their laps and can scent their
lavender scent, the cloud of hair that falls
over you, feel their feet trailing in the river,
or hidden in a purse walk the Neva again. Best of all
you are used badly like a bouquet of flowers to make
them shed their dresses in apartments. See those
steam pipes running along the ceiling. The rope.

3

I wanted to feel exalted so I picked up
Doctor Zhivago again. But the newspaper was there
with the horrors of the Olympics, those dead and
perpetually martyred sons of David. I want to present
all Israelis with .357 magnums so that they are
never to be martyred again. I wanted to be exalted
so I picked up *Doctor Zhivago* again but the TV was on
with a movie about the sufferings of convicts in
the early history of Australia. But then the movie
was over and the level of the bourbon bottle was dropping
and I still wanted to be exalted lying there with
the book on my chest. I recalled Moscow but I could
not place dear Yuri, only you Yesenin, seeing the Kremlin
glitter and ripple like Asia. And when drunk you appeared
as some Bakst stage drawing, a slain Tartar. But that is
all ballet. And what a dance you had kicking your legs from
the rope—We all change our minds, Berryman said in Minnesota
halfway down the river. Villon said of the rope that my neck
will feel the weight of my ass. But I wanted to feel exalted
again and read the poems at the end of *Doctor Zhivago* and
just barely made it. Suicide. Beauty takes my courage
away this cold autumn evening. My year-old daughter's red
robe hangs from the doorknob shouting *Stop*.

4

I am four years older than you but scarcely an unwobbling
pivot. It was no fun sitting around being famous, was it?
I'll never have to learn that lesson. You find a page torn
out of a book and read it feeling that here you might find
the mystery of print in such phrases as "summer was on the
way" or "Gertrude regarded him somewhat quizzically." Your
Sagane was a fraud. Love poems to girls you never met living
in a country you never visited. I've been everywhere to no
particular purpose. And am well past love but not love poems.
I wanted to fall in love on the coast of Ecuador but the girls
were itsy-bitsy and showers are not prominent in that area.
Unlike Killarney where I also didn't fall in love the girls
had good teeth. As in the movies the Latin girls proved to be
spitfires with an endemic shanker problem. I didn't fall in love
in Palm Beach or Paris. Or London. Or Leningrad. I wanted to fall
in love at the ballet but my seat was too far back to see faces
clearly. At Sadko a pretty girl was sitting with a general
and did not exchange my glance. In Normandy I fell in love but
had colitis and couldn't concentrate. She had a way of not paying
any attention to me that could not be misunderstood. That is
a year's love story. Except Key West where absolutely nothing
happened with romantic overtones. Now you might understand why
I drink and grow fat. When I reach three hundred pounds there
will be no more love problems, only fat problems. Then I will
write reams of love poems. And if she pats my back a cubic yard

of fat will jiggle. Last night I drank a hundred-proof quart
and looked at a photo of my sister. Ten years dead. Show me a
single wound on earth that love has healed. I fed my dying dog
a pound of beef and buried her happy in the barnyard.

5

Lustra. Officially the cold comes from Manitoba;
yesterday at sixty knots. So that the waves mounted
the breakwater. The first snow. The farmers and carpenters
in the tavern with red, windburned faces. I am in there
playing the pinball machine watching all those delicious
lights flutter, the bells ring. I am halfway through
a bottle of vodka and am happy to hear Manitoba
howling outside. Home for dinner I ask my baby daughter
if she loves me but she is too young to talk. She cares
most about eating as I care most about drinking. Our wants
are simple as they say. Still when I wake from my nap
the universe is dissolved in grief again. The baby is sleeping
and I have no one to talk my language. My breath is shallow
and my temples pound. Vodka. Last October in Moscow I taught
a group of East Germans to sing "Fuck Nixon," and we were
quite happy until the bar closed. At the newsstand I saw a
picture of Bella Akhmadulina and wept. Vodka. You would have
liked her verses. The doorman drew near, alarmed. Outside
the KGB floated through the snow like arctic bats.
Maybe I belong there. They won't let me print my verses. On the
night train to Leningrad I will confess everything to someone.
All my books are remaindered and out of print. My face in
the mirror asks me who I am and says I don't know. But stop
this whining. I am alive and a hundred thousand acres of birches

around my house wave in the wind. They are women standing on their heads. Their leaves on the ground today are small saucers of snow from which I drink with endless thirst.

6

Fruit and butter. She smelled like the skin of an apple.
The sun was hot and I felt an unbounded sickness with earth.
A single October day began to last a year. You can't fuck
your life away, I thought. But you can! Listening in Nepal
to those peahens scream in the evening. Then, through the glade,
lordly he enters, his ass a ten-foot fan, a painting by a crazed
old master. Look, they are human. Heads the size of two knuckles.
But returning to her buttery appleness and autumn, my dead friend.
We cannot give our lives over to women. Kneeling there under that
vulgar sugar maple tree I couldn't breathe and with a hundred
variations of red above me and against my mouth. She said I'm
going away to Oregon perhaps. I said that I'm going myself to
California where I hear they sleep out every night. So that
ended that and the fan was tucked neatly and the peahens' screams
were heard no more in the land and old ladies and old men slept
soundly again and threw away their cotton earplugs and the earth
of course was soaked with salt and August passed without a single
ear of corn. Of course this was only one neighborhood. Universality
is disgusting. But you had your own truly insurmountable horrors
with that dancer, lacking all wisdom as you did. Your critic said
you were "often revolted by your sensuality." He means
all of that endless fucking of course. Tsk tsk. Put one measure
against another and how rarely they fuse, and how almost never is
there any fire and how often there is only boredom and a craving
for cigarettes, a sandwich, or a drink. Particularly a drink.

I am drunk because I no longer can love. I make love and I'm writing on a blackboard. Once it was a toteboard, a gun handle until I myself became a notch. And a notch, to be obvious, is a nothing. This all must pass as a monk's tale, a future lie.

7

Death thou comest when I had thee least in mind, said Everyman
years ago in England. Can't get around much anymore. So it's
really a terrible surprise unless like you we commit suicide.
I worry some that the rope didn't break your neck, but that
you dangled there strangling from your body's weight. Such
physics can mean a rather important matter of three or four
minutes. Then I would guess there was a moment of black peacefulness
then you were hurtling in space like a mortar. Who can say
if a carcass smiles, if the baggage is happy at full rest. The
child drowns in a predictable puddle or inside the plastic bag
from which you just took your tuxedo. The evening is certainly
ruined and we can go on from there but that too is predictable.
I want to know. I have no explanations for myself but if someone
told me that my sister wasn't with Jesus they would get an
ass-kicking. There's a fascinating tumor called a melanoma
that apparently draws pigment from surrounding tissue until
it's black as coal. That fatal lump of coal tucked against the
spine. And of all things on earth a bullet can hit human
flesh is one of the least resistant. It's late autumn and this
is an official autumnal mood, a fully sanctioned event in which
one may feel the thrill of victory and the agony of defeat. But
as poets we would prefer to have a star fall on us (that meteor
got me in the gizzard!), or lightning strike us and not while we're
playing golf but perhaps in a wheat field while we're making
love in a thunderstorm, or a tornado take us away outside of

Mingo, Kansas, like Judy Garland unfortunately. Or a rainbow
suffocate us. Or skewered dueling the mighty forces of anti-
art. Maybe in sleep as a Gray Eminence. A painless sleep of course.
Or saving a girl from drowning who turns out to be a mermaid.

8

I cleaned the granary dust off your photo with my shirtsleeve.
Now that we are tidy we can wait for the host to descend
presumably from the sky as that seems to exhaust the alternatives.
You had a nice summer in the granary. I was out there with you
every day in June and July writing one of my six-week wonders,
another novel. Loud country music on the phonograph, wasps
and bees and birds and mice. The horses looked in the window
every hour or so, curious and rather stupid. Chief Joseph stared
down from the wall at both of us, a far nobler man than
we ever thought possible. We can't lead ourselves and he led
a thousand with a thousand horses a thousand miles. He was a god
and had three wives when one is usually more than enough for
a human. These past weeks I have been organizing myself into
my separate pieces. I have the limberness of a man twice my age
and this is as good a time as any to turn around. Joseph was
very understanding, incidentally, when the cavalry shot so many
of the women and children. It was to be expected. Earth is
full of precedents. They hang around like underground trees
waiting for their chance. The fish swam around four years solid
in preparation for August the seventh, 1972, when I took his life
and ate his body. Just as we may see our own ghosts next to
us whose shapes we will someday flesh out. All of this suffering
to become a ghost. Yours held a rope, manila, straight from
the tropics. But we don't reduce such glories to a mudbath.
The ghost giggles at genuflections. You can't buy him a drink.

Out in a clearing in the woods the other day I got up on a stump and did a little dance for mine. We know the most frightening time is noon. The evidence says I'm halfway there, such wealth I can't give away, thirty-four years of seconds.

9

What if I own more paper clips than I'll ever use in this
lifetime? My other possessions are shabby: the house half-
painted, the car without a muffler, one dog with bad eyes
and the other dog a horny moron. Even the baby has a rash on
her neck but then we don't own humans. My good books were
stolen at parties long ago and two of the barn windows are
broken and the furnace is unreliable and field mice daily
feed on the wiring. But the new foal appears healthy though
unmanageable, crawling under the fence and chased by my wife
who is stricken by the flu, not to speak of my own body which
has long suffered the ravages of drink and various nervous
disorders that make me laugh and weep and caress my shotguns.
But paper clips. Rich in paper clips to sort my writings which
fill so many cartons under the bed. When I attach them I say
it's your job after all to keep this whole thing together. And
I used them once with a rubber band to fire holes into the
face of the president hanging on the office wall. We have freedom.
You couldn't do that to Brezhnev much less Stalin on whose
grave Mandelstam sits proudly in the form of the ultimate
crow, a peerless crow, a crow without comparison on earth.
But the paper clips are a small comfort like meeting someone
fatter than myself and we both wordlessly recognize the fact
or meeting someone my age who is more of a drunk, more savaged
and hag-ridden until they are no longer human and seeing
them on the street I wonder how their heads which are only

wounds balance on the top of their bodies. A manuscript of
a novel sits in front of me held together with twenty clips.
It is the paper equivalent of a duck and a company far away
has bought this perhaps beautiful duck and my time is free again.

10

It would surely be known for years after as the day I shot
a cow. Walking out of the house before dawn with the sky an icy
blackness and not one star or cockcrow or shiver of breeze, the rifle
barrel black and icy to the touch. I walked a mile in the dark
and a flushed grouse rose louder than any thunderclap. I entered
a neck of a woodlot I'd scouted and sat on a stump waiting for
a deer I intended to kill. But then I was dressed too warmly
and had a formidable hangover with maybe three hours of sleep so
I slept again seeing a tin open-fronted café in Anconcito down
on the coast of Ecuador and the eyes of a piglet staring at me as
I drank my mineral water dazed with the opium I had taken for
la turista. Crippled syphilitic children begging, one little boy
with a tooth as long as a forefinger, an ivory tusk which would
be pulled on maturity and threaded as an amulet ending up finally
in Moscow in a diplomatic pouch. The boy would explore with his
tongue the gum hole for this Russian gift. What did he know about
Russia. Then carrying a naked girl in the water on my shoulders
and her short hairs tickled the back of my neck with just the suggestion
of a firm grip behind them so if I had been stupid enough to turn
around I might have suffocated at eighteen and not written you
any letters. There were bristles against my neck and hot breath
in my hair. It must be a deer smelling my hair so I wheeled and shot.
But it was a cow and the muzzle blast was blue in the gray light.
She bawled horribly and ran in zigzags. I put her away with a shot
to the head. What will I do with this cow? It's a guernsey and she

won't be milked this morning. I knelt and stared into her huge eyeball, her iris making a mirror so I combed my hair and thought about the whole dreary mess. Then I walked backward through a muddy orchard so I wouldn't be trailed, got in my car and drove to New York nonstop.

11

for Diane W.

No tranquil pills this year wanting to live peeled as they
described the nine throats of Cerberus. Those old greek names
keep popping up. You can tell we went to college and our sleep
is troubled. There are geographical equivalents for exotic tropes
of mind; living peeled was the Arizona Inn in Tucson talking with D.W.
about love and art with so much pain my ears rang and the breath
came short. And outside the fine desert air wasn't fine anymore:
the indians became kachina dolls and a girl was tortured daily
for particular reasons. This other is our Akhmatova and often we want
to hide from her—seasoned as she is in so many hells. But why paint
her for one of the dead who knew her pungency of love, the unforgivable
low-tide smell of it, how few of us bear it for long before reducing
it to a civil act. You were odd for a poet attaching yourself
to a woman no less a poet than yourself. It still starts with
the dance. In the end she probably strangled you and maybe back
in Ryazan there was a far better bird with less extravagant plumage.
But to say I'm going to spend the day thinking wisely about
women is to say I'm going to write an indomitably great poem before
lunch or maybe rule the world by tomorrow dawn. And I couldn't
love one of those great SHES—it's far too late and they are far
too few to find anyway though that's a driveling excuse. I saw one
in a tree and on a roof. I saw one in a hammock and thigh-deep
in a pond. I saw one out in the desert and sitting under a willow

by the river. All past tense you notice and past haunting but not past caring. What did she do to you and did you think of her when your terrible shadow fell down the wall. I see that creature sitting on the lawn in Louveciennes, the mistress of a superior secret. We have both died from want of her, cut off well past our prime.

12

I was proud at four that my father called me Little Turd of Misery.
A special name somehow connected to all the cows and horses in
the perpetual mire of the barnyard. It has a resonance to it un-
known to president senator poet septic-tank cleaner critic butcher
hack or baker liberal or snot, rightist and faker and faggot and
cunt hound. A child was brought forth and he was named Little Turd
of Misery and like you was thrown into the lake to learn how to
swim, owned dogs that died stupidly but without grief. Why does
the dog chase his broken legs in a circle? He almost catches them
like we almost catch our unruly poems. And our fathers and uncles
had ordinary pursuits, hunted and fished, smelled of tobacco and
liquor, grew crops, made sauerkraut and wine, wept in the dark,
chased stray cows, mended fences, were hounded as they say by
creditors. Barns burned. Cabbages rotted. Corn died of drought
before its holy ears were formed, wheat flattened by hail and wind and
the soup grew only one potato and a piece of salt pork from its
center. Generations of slavery. All so we could fuck neurotically
and begin the day rather than end it drinking and dreaming of dead
dogs, swollen creeks with small bridges, ponds where cows are caught
and drown, sucked in by the muck. But the wary boy catches fish
there, steals a chicken for his dog's monthly birthday, learns
to smoke, sees his first dirty picture and sings his first dirty
song, goes away, becomes deaf with song, becomes blinded by love,
gets letters from home but never returns. And his nights become
          less black

and holy, less moon-blown and sweet. His brain burns away like
gray paraffin. He's tired. His parents are dead or he is dead
to his parents. He smells the smell of a horse. The room is
cold. He dims the light and builds a noose. It works too well.

13

All of those little five-dollar-a-week rooms smelling thick of
cigarette smoke and stale tea bags. The private bar of soap
smearing the dresser top, on the chair a box of cookies and a letter
from home. And what does he think he's doing and do we all begin our
voyage into Egypt this way? The endless bondage of words. That's why
you turned to those hooligan taverns and vodka, Crane to his
sailors in Red Hook. Four walls breathe in and out. The clothes on
the floor are a dirty shroud. The water is stale in its glass.
Just one pull on the bottle starts the morning faster. If you
don't rouse your soul you will surely die while others are having
lunch. Noon. You passed the point of retreat and took that dancer,
a goad, perhaps a goddess. The food got better anyhow and the
bottles. This is all called romantic by some without nostrils
tinctured by cocaine. No romance here, but a willingness to age
and die at the speed of sound. Outside there's a successful revolution
and you've been designated a parasite. Everywhere crushed women
are bearing officious anti-Semites. Stalin begins his diet of
iron shavings and blood. Murder swings with St. Basil's bell, a
thousand per gong free of charge. North on the Baltic Petrodvorets
is empty and inland, Pushkin is empty. Nabokov has sensibly flown
the shabby coop. But a hundred million serfs are free and own
more than the common bread; a red-tinged glory, neither fire nor
sun, a sheen without irony on the land. Who could care that you
wanted to die, that your politics changed daily, that your songs
turned to glass and were broken? No time to marry back in Ryazan,

buy a goat, three dogs, and fish for perch. The age gave you a
pistol and you gave it back, gave you two wives and you gave
them both back, gave you a rope to swing from which you used wisely.
You were good enough to write that last poem in blood.

14

Imagine being a dog and never knowing what you're doing. You're
simply *doing*: eating garbage, fawning, mounting in public with
terrible energy. But let's not be romantic. Those curs, however
sweet, don't have souls. For all of the horrors at least some of
us have better lives than dogs. Show me a dog that ever printed
a book of poems read by no one in particular before he died at
seventeen, old age for a dog. No dog ever equaled Rimbaud for
grace or greatness, for rum running, gun running, slave trading
and buggery. The current phrase, "anything that gets you off,"
includes dogs but they lack our catholicity. Still, Sergei, we never
wanted to be dogs. Maybe indians or princes, Caesars or Mongolian
chieftains, women in expensive undergarments. But if women, lesbians
to satisfy our ordinary tastes for women. In a fantasy if you
become a woman you quickly are caressing your girlfriend. That
pervert. I never thought she would. Be like that. When she's away
from me. Back to consciousness, the room smells like a locker room.
Out the window it's barely May in Moscow and the girls have shed
their winter coats. One watches a group of fishermen. She has
green eyes and is recent from the bath. If you were close enough
which you'll never be you could catch her scent of lemon and
the clear softness of her nape where it meets her hair. She'll
probably die of flu next year or marry an engineer. The same
things really as far as you're concerned. And it's the same in this
country. A fine wife and farm, children, animals, three good reviews.
Then a foggy day in late March with dozens of crows in the air

and a girl on a horse passes you in the woods. Your dog barks. The girl stops, laughing. She has green eyes. Your heart is off and running. Your groin hopes. You pray not to see her again.

15

The soul of water. The most involved play. She wonders if she
is permitted to name the stars. Tell her no. This month, May,
is said to be "the month of tiny plant-sucking pests." So even
nature is said to war against us though those pests it seems are
only having lunch. So the old woman had named the stars above
her hut and wondered if god had perhaps given them other names that
she didn't know about. Her priest was always combing his hair
and shining his shoes. We were driven from the church, weren't we
Sergei? In hearses. But is this time for joking? Yes. Always.
We wonder if our fathers in heaven or hell watch when we are about
our lying and shameful acts. As if they up or down there weren't
sick enough of life without watching for eternity some faulty
version of it, no doubt on a kind of TV. Tune the next hour out
dad, I'm going to be bad. Six lines of coke and a moronic twitch.
Please don't watch. I can't help myself. I provide for my children.
They're delighted with the fish I catch. My wife smiles hourly.
She has her horses, dogs, cat, barn, garden. But in New York twenty
layers above the city some cloud or stratum of evil wants to enter
me and I'm certainly willing. Even on ground level in Key West.
Look she has no clothes on and I only wanted to be a friend and
maybe talk about art. Only a lamb. Of course this Little Boy Blue
act is tiresome and believed by no one on earth, heaven or hell.
So we've tried to name the stars and think we are forgiven in
advance. Rimbaud turned to black or arab boys remembering when he
was twelve and there was no evil. Only a helpless sensual wonder.

Pleasure gives. And takes. It is dark and hot and the brain is howling with those senseless drugs. Mosquitoes land upon those fields of sweat, the pool between her breasts. You want to be home rocking your child in a sunny room. Now that it's over. But wait.

16

Today we've moved back to the granary again and I've anointed
the room with *Petrouchka*. Your story, I think. And music. That
ends with you floating far above in St. Petersburg's blue winter
air, shaking your fist among the fish and green horses, the dim-
inutive yellow sun and chicken playing the bass drum. Your
sawdust is spilled and you are forever borne by air. A simple story.
Another madman, Nijinsky, danced your part and you danced his.
None of us apparently is unique. Think of dying waving a fist full
of ballpoint pens that change into small snakes and that your
skull will be transposed into the cymbal it was always meant to be.
But shall we come down to earth? For years I have been too ready
to come down to earth. A good poet is only a sorcerer bored with
magic who has turned his attention elsewhere. O let us see wonders
that psilocybin never conceived of in her powdery head. Just now
I stepped on a leaf that blew in the door. There was a buzzing
and I thought it concealed a wasp, but the dead wasp turned out to be
a tiny bird, smaller than a hummingbird or june bug. Probably one
of a kind and I can tell no one because it would anger the swarm
of naturalists so vocal these days. I'll tuck the body in my hair
where it will remain forever a secret or tape it to the back of
your picture to give you more depth than any mirror on earth.
And another oddity: the record needle stuck just at the point
the trumpet blast announced the appearance of your ghost in the
form of Petrouchka. I will let it repeat itself a thousand times
through the afternoon until you stand beside the desk in your

costume. But I've no right to bring you back to life. We must respect your affection for the rope. You knew the exact juncture in your life when the act of dangling could be made a dance.

17

Behind my back I have returned to life with much more surprise
than conviction. All those months in the cold with neither
tears nor appetite no matter that I was in Nairobi or Arusha, Rome,
the fabled Paris flat and dry as a newsphoto. And lions looked
like lions in books. Only the rumbling sound of an elephant shooting
water into his stomach with a massive trunk made any sense. But I
thought you would have been pleased with the Galla women in Ethiopia
and walking the Colonnade near the Vendôme. I knew you had walked
there. Such a few signs of life. Life brings us down to earth he
thinks. Father of two at thirty-five can't seem to earn a living.
But whatever muse there is on earth is not concerned with groceries.
We like to believe that Getty couldn't buy a good line for a billion
dollars. When we first offered ourselves up to her when young and
in our waking dreams she promised nothing. Not certainly that we
could buy a bike for our daughter's birthday or eat good cuts of
beef instead of hamburger. She doesn't seem to care that our wine
is ordinary. She walks in and out the door without knocking. She takes
off her clothes and ruins the marriage bed. She out-and-out killed
you Sergei for no reason I can think of. And you might want to
kill her but she changes so fast whether into a song, a deer, a pig,
the girl sitting on the pier in a short dress. You want to fish
but you turn and there larger than any movie are two thighs and louder
than any howl they beckon you to the life they hold so gently. We
said that her eyes were bees and ice glistened in her hair. And we
know she can become a rope but then you're never sure as all rope

tends to resemble itself though it is common for it to rest in coils like snakes. Or rope. But I must earn our living and can't think about rope though I am to be allowed an occasional girl drawing up her thighs on a pier. You might want her even in your ghostly form.

18

Thus the poet is a beached gypsy, the first porpoise to whom it
occurred to commit suicide. True, my friend, even porpoises have
learned your trick and for similar reasons: losing hundreds of
thousands of wives, sons, daughters, husbands to the tuna nets.
The seventh lover in a row disappears and it can't be endured.
There is some interesting evidence that Joplin was a porpoise and
simply decided to stop breathing at an unknown depth. Perhaps the
navy has her body and is exploring ways to turn it into a weapon.
Off Boca Grande a baby porpoise approached my boat. It was a girl
about the size of my two-year-old daughter who might for all I know
be a porpoise. Anyway she danced around the boat for an hour
while her mother kept a safer distance. I set the mother at ease by
singing my infamous theme song: "Death dupe dear dingle devil flower
bird dung girl," repeating seven times until the mother approached
and I leaned over the gunnel and we kissed. I was tempted to swim
off with them but remembered I had a date with someone who tripled
as a girl, cocaine dealer and duck though she chose to be the last,
alas, that evening. And as in all ancient stories I returned to the
spot but never found her or her little girl again. Even now mariners
passing the spot deep in the night can hear nothing. But enough
of porpoise love. And how they are known to beach themselves. I've
begun to doubt whether we ever would have been friends. Maybe. Not
that it's to the point—I know three one-eyed poets like myself
but am close to none of them. These letters might have kept me
alive—something to do you know as opposed to the nothing you chose.

Loud yeses don't convince. Nietzsche said you were a rope dancer before you were born. I say yes before breakfast but to the smell of bacon. Wise souls move through the dark only one step at a time.

19

Naturally we would prefer seven epiphanies a day and an earth
not so apparently devoid of angels. We become very tired with
pretending we like to earn a living, with the ordinary objects and
events of our lives. What a beautiful toothbrush. How wonderful
to work overtime. What a nice cold we have to go with the cold
crabbed spring. How fun to have no money at all. This thin soup
tastes great. I'm learning something every morning from cheap wine
hangovers. These rejection slips are making me a bigger person.
The mailbox is always so empty let's paint it pink. It's good for
my soul that she prefers to screw another. Our cat's right eyeball
became ulcerated and had to be pulled but she's the same old cat.
I can't pay my taxes and will be sent to prison but it will probably
be a good experience. That rattlesnake striking at dog and daughter
was interesting. How it writhed beautifully with its head cut
off and dog and daughter were tugging at it. How purging to lose
our last twenty dollars in a crap game. Seven come eleven indeed.
But what grand songs you made out of an awful life though you had
no faith that less was more, that there was some golden splendor
in humiliation. After all those poems you were declared a coward
and a parasite. Mayakovsky hissed in public over your corpse and
work only to take his own life a little while later. Meanwhile
back in America Crane had his Guggenheim year and technically jumped
ship. Had he been seven hundred feet tall he would have been OK.
I suspect you would have been the kind of friends you both needed
so badly. So many husbands have little time for their homosexual

friends. But we should never imagine we love this daily plate of shit.
The horses in the yard bite and chase each other. I'll make a carol
of my dream: carried in a litter by lovely women, a 20 lb. bag of cocaine,
angels shedding tunics in my path, all dead friends come to life again.

20

The mushrooms helped again: walking hangdoggedly to the granary
after the empty mailbox trip I saw across the barnyard at the base
of an elm stump a hundred feet away a group of white morels. How
many there were will be kept concealed for obvious reasons. While
I plucked them I considered each a letter from the outside world
to my little cul-de-sac, this valley: catching myself in this act
doing what I most despise, throwing myself in the laps of others.
Save my life. Help me. By return post. That sort of thing. So we
throw ourselves in the laps of others until certain famous laps
grow tired, vigorous laps whose movement is slowed by the freight
of all those cries. Then if you become famous after getting off
so many laps you can look at the beautiful women at your feet and
say I'll take that foot and that breast and that thigh and those lips
you have become so denatured and particular. They float and merge
their parts trying to come up with something that will please you.
Selecting the finest belly you write your name with a long thin
line of cocaine but she is perspiring and you can't properly snort
it off. Disappointments. The belly weeps but you dismiss her, sad
and frightened that your dreams have come to no end. Why cast Robert
Redford in your life story if all that he's going to do is sit there
and piss and moan at the typewriter for two hours in expensive
Eastman color? Not much will happen if you don't like to drink
champagne out of shoes. And sated with a half-dozen French meals a day
you long for those simple boiled potatoes your estranged wife made
so perfectly. The letters from your children are defiled in a stack

of fan mail and obscene photos. Your old dog and horse have been given to kindly people and your wife will soon marry a jolly farmer. No matter that your million-selling books are cast in bronze. On a whim you fly to Palm Beach, jump on your yacht and set the automatic. You fit a nylon hawser around your neck, hurl overboard, and after the sharks have lunch your head skips in the noose like a marlin bait.

21

To answer some of the questions you might ask were you alive and
had we become friends but what do poets ask one another after long
absence? How have you been other than dead and how have I been
dying on earth without naming the average string of complaints which
is only worrying aloud, naming the dreaded motes that float around
the brain, those pink balloons calling themselves poverty, failure,
sickness, lust, and envy. To mention a very few. But you want part-
iculars, not the human condition or a letter to the editor on why
when I'm at my worst I think I've been fucked over. So here's this
Spring's news: now that the grass is taller I walk in some fear of
snakes. Feeling melancholy I watched my wife plant the garden row
on row while the baby tried to catch frogs. It's hard not to eat too
much when you deeply love food but I've limited myself to a half
gallon of burgundy a day. On long walks my eyes are so sunk back
in my brain they see nothing, then move forward again toward the light
and see a high meadow turning pale green and swimming in the fog
with crows tracing perceptible and geometrical paths just above
the fog but audible. At the shore I cast for fish, some of them
large with deliquescing smelt and alewives in their bellies. Other
than marriage I haven't been in love for years; close calls over
the world I mentioned to you before, but it's not love if it isn't
a surprise. I look at women and know deeply they are from another
planet and sometimes even lightly touching a girl's arm I know
I am touching a lovely though alien creature. We don't get back
those days we don't caress, don't make love. If I could get you out

in the backcountry down in Key West and get some psilocybin into you you would cut your legendary vodka consumption. Naturally I still believe in miracles and the holy fate of the imagination. How is it being dead and would I like it and should I put it off for a while?

22

These last few notes to you have been a bit somber like biographies
of artists written by joyless people so that the whole book is
a record of agony at thirty rather than thirty-three and a third.
You know the sound—Keeeaaattts wuzzz verrry unhapppppppy abouttt
dyinnnng. So here are some of those off-the-wall extravagancies.
Dawn in Ecuador with mariachi music, dawn at Ngorongoro with
        elephants
far below in the crater swaggering through the marsh grass, dawn in
Moscow and snowing with gold minarets shouting that you have at last
reached Asia, dawn in Addis Ababa with a Muslim waver in the cool
air smelling of ginger and a lion roaring on the lawn, dawn in
bleary Paris with a roll tasting like zinc and a girl in a cellophane
blouse staring at you with four miraculous eyes, dawn in Normandy
with a conceivable princess breathing in the next room and horses
wandering across the moat beneath my window, dawn in Montana with
herons calling from the swamp, dawn in Key West wondering if it was
a woman or tarpon that left your bed before cockcrow, dawn at home
when your eyes are molten and the ghost of your dog chases the fox
across the pasture, dawn on the Escanaba with trout dimpling the
mist and the water with a dulcet roar, dawn in London when the party-
girl leaves your taxi to go home to Shakespeare, dawn in Leningrad
with the last linden leaves falling and you knocking at the door
for a drunken talk but I am asleep. Not to speak of the endless and
nearly unconscious water walks after midnight when even the stars
might descend another foot to get closer to earth. Heat. The wetness

of air. Couplings. Even the mosquitoes are lovely and seem to imitate miniature birds. And a lion's cough is followed rhythmically by a hyena's laugh to prove that nature loves symmetry. The black girl leaves the grand hotel for her implausibly shabby home. The poet had dropped five sorts of drugs in his belly swill of alcohol and has imagined his deathless lines commemorating your last

      Leningrad night.

23

I want to bother you with some recent nonsense; a classmate dropped
dead, his heart was attacked at thirty-three. At the crematory
they lowered his body by fire-resistant titanium cables reminding
one of the steak on a neglected barbecue grill, only more so. We're
not supposed to believe that the vase of ashes is the real him.
You can imagine the mighty roar of the gas jets, a train coming
closer, the soul of thunder. But this is only old hat, or old death,
whichever. "Pause here, son of sorrow, remember death," someone once
said. "We can't have all things here to please us, our little Sue Ann
is gone to Jesus," reads an Alabama gravestone. But maybe even Robert
Frost and Charles Olson don't know they are dead. That would include
you of course. It is no quantity, absolute zero, the air in a hole
minus its airiness, the vacuum from the passing bird or bullet, the
end of the stem where the peach was, the place above the ground
where the barn burned with such energy we plugged our ears. If not,
show yourself in ten minutes. Let's settle this issue because I feel
badly today: a sense that my teeth and body are rotting on the hoof.
I could avoid the whole thing with a few drinks—it's been over
eight hours—but I want to face it like Simon Magus or poor Faustus.
Nothing, however, presents itself other than that fading picture of
my sister with an engine in her lap, not a very encouraging item
to be sure. I took Anna who is two for her first swim today. We didn't
know we were going swimming so she wore a pink dress, standing in
the lake up to her waist in wonderment. The gaucheries of children,
the way they love birds and neon lights, kill snakes and eat sand.

But I decided I wanted to go swimming for the first time and wanted to make love for the first time again. These thoughts can make you unhappy. Perhaps if your old dog had been in the apartment that night you wouldn't have done it. Everything's so fragile except ropes.

24

Dear friend. It rained long and hard after a hot week and when I
awoke the world was green and leafy again, or as J.D. says, everything
was new like a warm rain after a movie. And I said enough of death
and its obvious health hazards, it's a white-on-white jigsaw puzzle
in one piece. An hour with the doctor yesterday when he said my
blood pressure was so high I might explode as if I had just swallowed
an especially tasty grenade. I must warn my friends not to stand
too close. Blood can be poisonous; the Kikuyu in Kenya are often
infected when they burrow hacking away in the gut of an elephant.
Some don't come back. But doctors don't say such things, except
W.C. Williams. Just like your doctor when you were going batty, mine
said, "You must be distressed, you eat and drink and smoke far too
much. Cut out these things. The lab found lilacs and part of the
backbone of a garter snake or garter in your stool sample, and the
remnants of a hair ball. Do you chew your comb? We are checking to
see if it's your hair as there are possible criminal questions here.
Meanwhile get this thatch of expensive prescriptions filled and I
advise extensive psychiatric care. I heard your barking when I left
the room. How did you manage gout at your age?" My eyes misted
and I heard fiddle music and I looked up from page 86 in the June
Vogue where my old nemesis Lauren Hutton was staring at me in a
doctor's office in northern Michigan. This is Paul Bunyan country
Lauren. And how did I get gout? All of that fried salt and side
pork as a child. Humble fare. Quintuple heaps of caviar and decanters
of vodka at the Hotel Europa in Leningrad. *Tête de veau,* the brains,

tongue and cheeks of a calf. Side orders of *tripe à la mode de Caen*
sweetbreads with morels. Stewed kidneys and heart. Three-pound steaks
as snacks, five dozen oysters and three lobsters in Boston. A barrel
of nice gravy. Wild boar. Venison. Duck. Partridge. Pig's feet. But
you know, Sergei, I must eat these magical trifles to keep from
getting brainy and sad, to avoid leaving this physical world.

25

An afterthought to my previous note; we must closely watch any self-pity and whining. It simply isn't manly. Better by far to be a cowboy drinking rusty water, surviving on the maggots that unwittingly ate the pemmican in the saddlebags. I would be the Lone and I don't need no one said the cowpoke. Just a man and his horse against everything else on earth and horses are so dumb they run all day from flies never learning that flies are everywhere. Though in their violent motion they avoid the flies for a few moments. It's time again not to push a metaphor too far. But back again to the successful farmer who has his original hoe bronzed like baby shoes above the Formica mantelpiece—I earned what I got, nobody give me nothing he says. Pasternak said you probably didn't think death was the end of it all. Maybe you were only checking it out for something new to write about. We thieves of fire are capable of such arrogance when not otherwise occupied as real people pretending to be poet farmers, important writers, capable lovers, sports fops, regular guys, rock stars with tiny nonetheless appreciative audiences. But the self-pity and whining must stop. I forgot to add that at the doctor's an old woman called in to say that her legs had turned blue and she couldn't walk or hold her urine and she was alone. Try that one on. Thirty years ago I remember my mother singing *Hello Central, give me heaven, I think my daddy is there* about the usual little boy in a wartime situation. We forget about those actual people, certainly our ancestors and neighbors, who die in earnest. They called my dad, the county agent, and his friend a poor farmer was swinging like you only from a rafter in the barn from a hay rope. What to do with his strange children—their thin bodies, low brows and narrow eyes—who were my schoolmates. They're working in auto factories now and still voiceless. We are different in that we suffer and love, are bored, with our mouths open and must speak on occasion for those others.

26

Going in the bar last Sunday night I noticed that they were having
high-school graduation down the street. Caps and gowns. June and
mayflies fresh from the channel fluttering in the warm still air.
After a few drinks I felt jealous and wanted someone to say, "Best of
luck in your chosen field," or, "The road of life is ahead of you."
Remember your first trip to Moscow at nineteen? Everything was pos-
sible. You watched those noblewomen at the riding academy who would
soon be permanently unhorsed, something you were to have mixed
feelings about, what with the way poets suck up to and are attracted
to the aristocracy however gimcrack. And though the great Blok
welcomed you, you felt tentative, an unknown quantity, and remained
so for several years. But how quickly one goes from being unknown
and embarrassed to bored and arrogant, from being ignored to expecting
deference. From fleabag rooms to at least the Plaza. And the daydreams
and hustling, the fantasies and endless work that get you from one
to the other, only to discover that you really want to go home. Start
over with a new deck. But back home all the animals are dead, the
friends have disappeared and the fields gone to weed. The fish
have flown from the creeks and ponds and the birds have all drowned
or gone to China. No one knows you—they have little time for poetry
in the country, or in the city for that matter except for the minis-
trations of a few friends. Your name bobs up like a Halloween
apple and literature people have the vague feeling that they should read
you if they ever "catch up" on their reading. Once on a train I saw
a girl reading a book of mine but she was homely and I had a toothache

so I let the moment pass. What delicious notoriety. The journalist
said I looked like a bricklayer or beer salesman, not being fashion-
ably slender. But lately the sun shines through, the sweet release
of flinging these lines at the dead, almost like my baby Anna throw-
ing grain to the horses a mile away, in the far corner of the pasture.

27

I won my wings! I got all A's! We bought fresh fruit! The toilet
broke! Thus my life draws fuel ineluctably from triumph. Manic,
rainy June slides into July and I am carefully dressing myself in
primary colors for happiness. When the summer solstice has passed
you know you're finally safe again. That midnight surely dates
the year. "Look to your romantic interests and business investments,"
says the star hack in the newspapers. But what if you have neither?
Millions will be up to nothing. One of those pure empty days with
all the presence of a hole in the ground. The stars have stolen
twenty-four hours and vengeance is out of the question. But I'm
a three-peckered purple goat if you were tied to any planet by your
cord. That is mischief, an inferior magic; pulling the lining out
of a top hat. You merely rolled on the ground moaning trying to pull
that mask off but it had grown into your face. "Such a price the
gods exact for song to become what we sing," said someone. If it
aches that badly you have to take the head off, narrow the neck to
a third its normal size, a practice known as hanging by gift of the
state or as a do-it-yourself project. But what I wonder about is your
velocity: ten years from Ryazan to Leningrad. A little more than
a decade, two years into your fifth seven and on out like a proton
in an accelerator. You simply fell off the edge of the world while
most of us are given circles or, hopefully, spirals. The new
territory had a wall which you went over and on the other side there
was something we weren't permitted to see. Everyone suspects it's
nothing. Time will tell. But how you preyed upon, longed for, those

first ten years. We'll have to refuse that, however its freshness
in your hands. Romantic. Fatal. We learn to see with the child's
delight again or perish. We hope it was your vision you lost,
that before those final minutes you didn't find out something new.

28

to Robert Duncan

O to use the word *wingèd* as in bird or victory or airplane for
the first time. Not for spirit though, yours or anyone else's
or the bird that flew errantly into the car radiator. Or for poems
that sink heavily to our stomachs like fried foods, the powerful
ones, visceral, as impure as the bodies they flaunt. Curious what
you paid for your cocaine to get wingèd. We know the price of
the poems, one body and soul net, one brain already tethered to the
dark, one ingenious leash never to hold a dog, two midwinter eyes
that lost their technicolor. Think what you missed. Mayakovsky's
pistol shot. The Siege of Leningrad. Crows feasting on all of those
frozen German eyes. Good Russian crows that earned a meal putting
up with all of that insufferable racket of war. Curious crows watching
midnight purges, wary of owls, and the girl in the green dress
on the ground before a line of soldiers. She and the crow exchange
pitiless glances. She flaps her arms but is not wingèd. Maybe
there is one ancient crow that remembers the Czarina's jeweled
sleigh, the ring of its small gold bells; and the sickly wingèd
horse in the cellar of the Winter Palace, product of a mad breeding
experiment for eventual escape, how it was dumped into the Neva
before the talons grew through the hooves, the marvel of it lost
in the uproar of those days, the proof of it in the bones somewhere
on the floor of the Baltic delta. But we all get lost in the course
of empire, which lacks the Brownian movement's stability. We count
on iron men to stick to their guns. Our governments are weapons

of exhaustion. Poems fly out of yellow windows at night with a stall factor just under a foot, beneath our knees and the pre-Fourth of July corn in the garden. At least at that level radar can't detect them and they're safe from State interference. We know perfectly well you flapped your arms madly, unwingèd but craving a little flight.

29

We're nearing the end of this homage that often resembles a
suicide note to a suicide. I didn't mean it that way but how
often our hands sneak up on our throats and catch us unaware.
What are you doing here we say. Don't squeeze so hard. The hands
inside the vodka bottle and on the accelerator, needles and coke-
sore noses. It's not very attractive, is it? But now there is rain
on the tin roof, the world outside is green and leafy with bluebirds
this morning dive-bombing drowning worms from a telephone wire,
the baby laughing as the dog eats the thirty-third snake of the
summer. And the bodies on the streets and beaches. Girl bottoms!
Holy. Tummies in the sun! Very probably holy. Peach evidence almost
struggling for air! A libidinal stew that calls us to life however
ancient and basal. May they plug their lovely ears with their big
toes. God surely loves them to make them look that way and can I
do less than He at least in this respect. As my humble country
father said in our first birds-and-bees talk so many years ago: "That
thing ain't just to pee through." This vulgarity saves us as
certainly as our chauvinism. Just now in midafternoon I wanted
a tumbler of wine but John Calvin said, "You got up at noon. No wine
until you get your work done. You haven't done your exercises to
suppress the gut the newspaper says women find most disgusting.
The fence isn't mended and the neighbor's cow keeps crawling through
in the night, stealing the fresh clover you are saving for Rachel
the mare when she drops her foal." So the wine bottle remains
corked and Calvin slips through the floorboards to the crawl space

where he spends all of his time hating his body. Would these concerns have saved you? Two daughters and a wife. Children prop our rotting bodies with cries of *earn earn earn*. On occasion we are kissed. So odd in a single green month to go from the closest to so far from death.

30

The last and I'm shrinking from the coldness of your spirit: that
chill lurid air that surrounds great Lenin in his tomb as if we
had descended into a cloud to find on the catafalque a man who has
usurped nature, isn't dead any more than you or I are dead. Only
unlikely to meet and talk to our current forms. Today I couldn't
understand words so I scythed ragweed and goldenrod before it could
go to seed and multiply. I played with god imagining how to hold His
obvious scythe that caught you, so unlike the others, aware and
cooperative. Is He glad to help if we're willing? A boring question
since we're so able and ingenious. Sappho's sparrows are always
telling us that love will save us, some *other* will arrive to draw
us cool water, lie down with us in our private darkness and make
us well. I think not. What a fabulous lie. We've disposed of sparrows
and god, the death of color, those who are dominated by noon and
the vision of night flowing in your ears and eyes and down your
throat. But we didn't mean to arrive at conclusions. Fifty years are
only a moment between this granary and a hanged man half the earth
away. You are ten years younger than my grandmother Hulda who still
sings Lutheran hymns and watches the Muskegon River flow. In whatever
we do, we do damage to ourselves; and in those first images there
were always cowboys or cossacks fighting at night, murdered animals
and girls never to be touched; dozing with head on your dog's chest
you understand breath and believe in golden cities where you will
live forever. And that fatal expectancy—not comprehending that we
like our poems are flowers for the void. In those last days you

wondered why they turned their faces. Any common soul knew you
had consented to death, the only possible blasphemy. I write to
you like some half-witted, less courageous brother, unwilling to tease
those ghosts you slept with faithfully until they cast you out.

Postscript

At 8:12 AM all of the watches in the world are being wound.
Which is not quite the same thing as all of the guitars on earth
being tuned at midnight. Or that all suicides come after the mail-
man when all hope is gone. Before the mailman, watches are wound,
windows looked through, shoes precisely tied, tooth care, the
attenuations of the hangover noted. Which is not the same as
the new moon after midnight or her bare feet stepping slowly toward
you and the snake easing himself from the ground for a meal.
The world is so necessary. Someone must execute stray dogs and
free the space they're taking up. I can see people walking down
Nevsky Prospekt winding their watches before you were discovered
too far above the ground, that mystical space that was somewhere
occupied by a stray dog or a girl in an asylum on her hands
and knees. A hanged face turns slowly from a plum to a lump of
coal. I'm winding my watch in antipathy. I see the cat racing
around the yard in a fantasy of threat. She's preparing for
eventualities. She prizes the only prize. But we aren't the cats
we once were thousands of years ago. You didn't die with the
dignity of an animal. Today you make me want to tie myself to
a tree, stake my feet to earth herself so I can't get away. It didn't
come as a burning bush or pillar of light but I've decided to stay.

Return to Yesenin

25 years later

> For only in praising is my heart still mine, so violently
> do I know the world.
>
>   RAINER MARIA RILKE, Fragment of an Elegy,
>   *Appendix to Duino Elegies*

I forgot to say that at the moment of death Yesenin
stood there like a misty-eyed pioneer woman trying
to figure out what happened. Were the children
still in the burning barn with the bawling cows?
He was too sensitive for words, and the idea of a rope
was a wound he couldn't stop picking at. To step
back from this swinging man twisting clockwise
is to see how we mine ourselves too deeply,
that way down there we can break through the soul's
rock into a black underground river that sweeps us away.
To be frank, I'd rather live to feed my dogs,
knowing the world says *no* in ten thousand ways
and *yes* in only a few. The dogs don't need another
weeping Jesus on the cross of Art, strumming the scars
to keep them alive, tending them in a private
garden as if our night-blooming tumors were fruit.
I let you go for twenty years and am now only
checking to see that you are really dead. There was an urge
to put a few bullets through Nixon's coffin or a big,
sharp wooden stake, and a girl told me she just saw

Jimi Hendrix at an AIDS benefit in Santa Monica.
How could I disbelieve her when her nipples
were rosebuds, though you had to avoid the snakes
in her hair. If you had hanged yourself in Argentina
you would have twisted counterclockwise. We can't
ask if it was worth it, can we? Any more than we can
ask a whale its mother's name. Too bad we couldn't
go to Mexico together and croak a few small gods
back to life. I've entered my third act and am
still following my songs on that thin line between
woods and field, well short of the mouth of your hell.

About the Author

Jim Harrison is the author of twenty-nine books, including *Legends of the Fall* and *Dalva,* and was for many years a food columnist for the magazines *Smart* and *Esquire*. His work has been produced as four feature-length films and translated into two dozen languages. Mr. Harrison divides his time between Montana and southern Arizona.

The Chinese character for poetry is made up of two parts: "word" and "temple." It also serves as pressmark for Copper Canyon Press.

Since 1972, Copper Canyon Press has fostered the work of emerging, established, and world-renowned poets for an expanding audience. The Press thrives with the generous patronage of readers, writers, booksellers, librarians, teachers, students, and funders—everyone who shares the belief that poetry is vital to language and living.

Major funding has been provided by:

Anonymous (2)

The Paul G. Allen Family Foundation

Beroz Ferrell & The Point, LLC

Lannan Foundation

National Endowment for the Arts

Cynthia Lovelace Sears and Frank Buxton

Washington State Arts Commission

THE **PAUL G. ALLEN FAMILY** *foundation*

NATIONAL
ENDOWMENT
FOR THE ARTS

WASHINGTON
STATE ARTS
COMMISSION

For information and catalogs:

COPPER CANYON PRESS
Post Office Box 271
Port Townsend, Washington 98368
360-385-4925
www.coppercanyonpress.org

Copper Canyon Classics re-presents essential, formative poetry texts in an affordable format. This book is set in Legacy Serif, a font designed by American type designer Ronald Arnholm after close study of Nicholas Jenson's 1470 Eusebius. Display type set in Reminga Titling, designed by Xavier Dupré. Book design and composition by Valerie Brewster, Scribe Typography.

Copper Canyon
Classics